AF265493

Songs Of My Heart

Songs Of My Heart
A Collection

Maureen Aisling Duffy-Boose

Copyright 2013 Maureen Aisling Duffy-Boose
All rights reserved. No part of this book may be used or reproduced in any manner whatsoever without written permission, except in the case of brief quotations embodied in critical articles or reviews.
Published 2011 by PPP Publications
All illustrations copyright 2013 PPP Publications
Front cover illustration M. Duffy-Boose and Geraldine Moorkens Byrne.
Illustrations M. Duffy-Boose
(EXC Feast - Geraldine Moorkens Byrne)
Copyright PPP Publications
21-22 Lower Stephen Street, Dublin 2, Ireland
Printed 2011 by Lulu.com in the United States of America

ISBN 978-0-9562403-2-3

This book is dedicated to my beloved wife Brie, my amazing children and grandchildren, and my mother, Mary Duffy, who first taught my heart to sing.

My deepest and heartfelt thanks to my editor and publisher, and dear friend, Geraldine Moorkens Byrne; and to all those who assisted me in learning to write and shepherded me through the publishing process.

Contents

Songs of my heart

Foreword

It is a great pleasure for me to present this collection from Maureen Aisling Duffy-Boose; both as an editor and as a fan. Maureen's collection is the third from PPP Publishing, and one that we pursued as a project from the very first. Her talent as a musician and her unerring ear for lyrical and emotive expression is something I have admired for a long time, and it confers a unique style on her poetry.

She brings a compassionate but honest eye to issues of politics and social justice; like the Celtic Filí she understands what it is to stand outside, to occupy the precarious position of groundbreaker. And like a Filí she bends the word to all its meanings and challenges the reader to draw out their own.

For the purposes of this collection her poetry has been divided into three main themes. **Hand in Hand by the Hearth** brings together her poetry of Love and Family; **My Heart Breaks** is a collection of her political and social poetry; and the eponymous **Songs of my Heart** gathers together the bulk of her poems ranging from spirituality and deity to music and nature. Like an Irish triad of old, the three main concerns of this modern bard spring most definitely from one unifying source - her heart.

Geraldine Moorkens Byrne

Geraldine is a founding editor of the PPP poetry site, and of PPP Publishing; she is also co-editor of the anthology Pagan Paeans.
Her work has been published in a variety of anthologies, collections and print publications including Where the Hazel Falls (anthology) and Asian Geographic (tribes edition, magazine); her work has also been performed as theatre.

About the Author

Maureen Aisling Duffy-Boose is a lifelong writer of fiction, poetry, newspaper journalism, and essays. She has been writing and teaching since she was a teenager, and is now retired from the teaching profession and enjoying her time as a grandmother of 16.

Maureen describes herself as a Pagan and Gay-Rights activist, Traditional Irish Craft Priestess, and resident of the incredible diversity and beauty of the Salt Lake Valley in Utah. She is a professional Celtic Harpist and is currently recording a CD of original Irish Harp compositions. Ms. Duffy-Boose is the author of two forthcoming children's books, and her first novel is to be published in 2013.

Hand in Hand by the Hearth

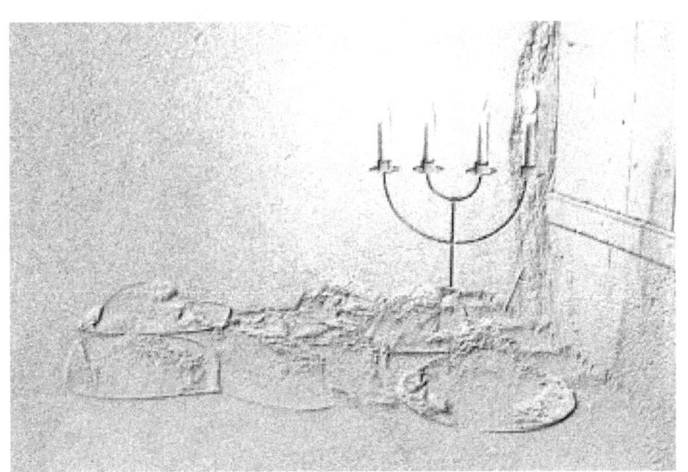

Birthday ~ For Brie

You were born today....
Your beauty came to the earth in an April shower,
And the loveliness of the woman you are
And were to be
Was hidden,
As now in our yard the roses
Are hidden beneath dead canes
And blown leaves,
Beauty that is to be
And was,
But is not yet.

You are my love
And every day, it seems to me,
Should be your birthday.
For there are never enough days,
Enough words,
Enough gifts
For me to let you know
How your very existence
Has brightened the bit of the world
Whereon I stand.

Somehow it is a cosmic rightness
That there be a day
That is all about you.
Every day of your life
Is all about others
And the imprint you leave on every thing, person, place you touch
Reminds me of sunlight
You cannot hold it
You cannot gather it
In its real and lucent form
But without it
Nothing is, anywhere.

So I write,
Knowing my words are a pale simulacrum
Of who you are,
What you mean to me,
But I know
That even in trying to tell you,
I am more, better, fuller

Simply because you live,
Because you were born,
I am alive, I am better

In a very real sense
Your birthday
Is the day I was born.

April 26, 2007

To Beirn, On Her Birthday

A Sonnet For An Unknown Sister

It seems so odd to me we've never met
In any way but electronically
Because the more we correspond, I see
Some things that I have not related yet
To any realm of logic. I can try
To understand our similarities
As somehow accidental. Yet if these
Are catalogued, it seems to me that I
See congruence of talent, taste, and mind
That strike me as not mere coincidence.
We seem akin, not merely friends. And hence
What great delight it was for me to find,
That Monaghan' a name and line we share...
I knew there might be more than friendship there!

Bealtine, For Brie

This morning I woke up to find her sleeping
Curled up against my shoulder like a child.
The tangled hair across her cheeks was creeping
And her breathing gently stirred it as she smiled.
Her cheek against my shoulder like a pillow
Nestled close and warm in peace and utter trust
And as I stirred, she murmured, cuddled closer,
And I turned to hold her close, because I must.

I held her gently, and I felt her muscles
Throb lithe and lean beneath my stroking hand,
And the satin skin as sleek as sleeping panther
Made my breathing come more rapid than I'd planned...
Caresses did not serve to wake her slumbers,
But only made her body cling more near,
And as my cheek was nestled on her forehead
A sudden truth came swift and crystal-clear...

It's not about the panting and the passion,
Or the cries of wild, abandoned ecstasy...
Instead, our Bealteine shows itself this fashion,
In the way her sleeping body clings to me...
That hollow right between my neck and shoulder
Where she rests her head at end of weary day,
And the way we'll finish each the other's sentence
And see the world in just the other's way...

It's here each morning that we honor Bealteine,
Nestled close in peace and love that knows no fear
Her eyes a hazel sunrise when she sees me
And "I love you" the first word we ever hear...
It's as I draw her closer in the evening
And she lays her weary cheek against my breast
And sighs as she wraps lissom legs around me
And relaxes to be cherished as we rest...

Ah, it was Bealteine, but I didn't wake her...
Instead, I wrapped my arms around her tight
And drifted off into a dream of loving
As I felt her close to me in sheer delight...
Forever we will have each other's waking
To every day of loving in our life
And every night will be another Bealteine
As I honor her, my Lady, Love and Wife!

With all my heart to my Goddess of Love
Bealteine 1997...first of a lifetime of loving!

It Was Like This *(form: Shadorma)*

When I fell
It wasn't gently
Romantic,
Beautiful,
Not at all like a love song.
Not a pretty sight.

In fact, I
Was clonked on the head
By her eyes,
By her smile,
In an instant of looking.
I didn't have time

To think it,
To understand it,
To repeat
To myself,
"Now you are falling in love,"
And feel it happen.

Oh, no. I
Was buried in love
In the one
Single look.
Hazel eyes, three-cornered smile
And now, she's my wife.

Immanence

I sit here, turning the tools in my hands,
Wishing to build something worthy of my love...
But what? What can I do,
Or say,
Or dream,
That can even begin to match the reality
Of who she is
And what she brings to me...

A poet, a rhyming trickster, I,
With much to say, of little substance;
And yet, now, for the first time,
I have material worthy the poet's pen,
And I cannot use it...
Every time I have tried
To tell her
Who she is to me,
What our love means to me,
I fall mute,
Frustrated by the wonder
Of the reality
Which so far surpasses the description...

Then I remembered...
Last night,
A sunset,
A rainbow,
The power of a stormwind...
Incredible beauty, fleeting as a breath,
Indescribable,
Changing even as we gazed...
"Oh, LOOK"...but when one did look,
The wonder was different...and one had missed that
Which drew forth the exclamation...
You just had to be there...

And I realized
That is how it is for me
There is never a moment
Empty of wonder,
Never a time when I could not
Write rapturous sonnets in her praise...
But the moments fleet by like flaming sunset clouds,
Wrapping me round with fleeting beauty,
And fading into other colors,
Other shapes,
Even as I gaze on what was just there...

I love you...
I love you as I love
The wonder of every varied moment of living...
You just have to be there.

Peeping

I sit here in my armchair
Gazing at your face
Smiling down from the wall at me
With your accustomed grace

Or sometimes, when you're busy
I just glance, unnoticed,

And you put me in a tizzy,
Even when you're fully focused
On whatever you are doing.

I can sneak a look and wonder
How long have you been brewing
The spell you have me under?

I fall away from my own work, uncaring
And watch the play of light
and shadow in your eyes...

It's always a surprise,
And always a delight,
To look when you don't see. How can I, daring

To disturb your concentration,
Even for a minute,

Intrude on you with talk of love
And how deep I am in it?

I love to rediscover how lovely you can be
while doing something focused,
that is nowise about me.

No matter how many times
I see you on the sofa
It is always a surprise that I never quite get over.

That you love me?!?

Then you look up
and give me that impish grin
and remind me once again, brand-new,
how deep the love I'm in...

No matter what you're doing, I can be
As stealthy as a cat, and turn my head
And try to see
What are you thinking? Watching? Doing?

But...It never fails...

You will look up at me,
as if I had just called your name, instead
Of silently

 just touching with my eyes...as if I touched, pursuing.
And love prevails.

You are forever somewhere, in your head
Or in a job of work...but I, unknown,
Can watch as if I were not there,
And know that you alone
Belong to me. On any day I gaze
You are within my view. The lamplight plays
Upon your hair, your skin...you have your work

But I....have you.

From a Picture

It's Monday.......

and I called you
Because I saw your face
Smiling down from the wall at me
With your accustomed grace
and that twinkle in your eyes...

The one that says it's I
you would most like to be looking at.

It's always a surprise,
That look.

No matter how many times
you give me that impish grin
and remind me once again
how deep the love I'm in...

No matter how you set the hook
And reel me in
To unsuspecting kisses...
I just sigh...

It never fails...

I always have to look
To be sure I am the one
You mean to give it to...

For when I look at you
I see beyond my wildest dreams

It's too good to be true...

And so it seems
I never can be good enough
To earn the prize I've won.

In fairy tales

it's always the most awkward boy
Who gets to kiss the princess...
So you can't blame me for wondering...

That look, that smile, those eyes...

Are they mine? Or is it just
You, a natural wonder
Shining down like starlight...
For whoever might be staring...

I'm past caring
whether it's for me.....
I only see
Your loveliness

And write...because you love me...
Or because you might.

Love on a Wednesday

It never gets old...
I walk down the halls of this house
and I feel your love for me beating in the walls
Like the blood through my veins.
I never get tired
Of feeling the energy of the love we share
surrounding me like the wall paper.

I walk into my office
And the first thing I see is you smiling at me,
more beautiful even than the view from the windows...
(Which is saying something!)
And I feel the reality
Of every dream I ever dared to dream in secret,
Knowing they were all fairy tales
And never expecting fulfillment.

It's just Wednesday
No special anniversary,
No day made for lovers...
Except that every day is that, now,
And I am among the privileged,
The ones who have someone to cherish,
Something to sing about...

And so I sit here,
And I know every word I say is inadequate
But in the face of beauty,
And love,
And the fulfillment of every waking dream,
How can I be silent
Even on a Wednesday?

Breaking My Heart

All I Can Do--Written for the 4th of July, 2011

All I can do is breathe in and out..
All I can do is be, and become, MySelf..
Every day,
Every moment,
Every interaction...

All I can do is try
Each and every time,
No matter how unsuccessful
The last time was,
I will not become mute,
I will try it again--
Same people.
Same audience.
Same old song.
I will sing it.

It's too easy
To look around
And wince, and cringe,
And want to bury my head
In the sands of Time,
Remembering.

Remembering a purer love of country,
Remembering when corporations were not persons,
Remembering when I got off the plane
From five years in Germany,
And literally got down on my knees,
And kissed the ground
Of my country--

It's not my country any more.
At least, it seems not to be.
The things I loved, the things for which I sang
"The Star-Spangled Banner",
Those things are no more...

I see money running everything,
I see politicians renewing the meaning of "poly-ticks",
As in myriads of bloodsucking insects.
I see those I have voted for
Not representing me and mine.
I see a war against women
I see a war against immigrants
I see a war against the environment

I see hate crimes against my religion and my sexuality.
I see the religious right trying to bring the country back
To our own dark ages, the time before there was
A Constitution and its Bill of Rights..

I could go on--but I haven't yet had coffee,
And thinking about all the darkness
That this weekend's fireworks cannot possibly illuminate
Is making me sick to my stomach.

So I am desolate.
Because I am only one woman,
With little political clout and power.
I am that person in the back row
Who sees the entire yard-tall wedding cake
Beginning to slip sideways
Whilst the bride and groom, oblivious,
Are toasting one another over the toppling cake
And I can't get there in time.

And so--
So, what can I do?
Nothing.
And everything.

Because all I can do
Is what I am doing.

I can speak out.
I can continue to vote
Not only in the ballot box,
But with my dollars,
And my feet,
And my words.

I am only one old woman.
But I see how beautiful this day is,
And last night's sunset,
Pale green and rose and navy
Over the Lake,
And my mountains
Where I go pick up trash
When I am there.

Sure, it's only three cigarette butts
And two cans, and a McDonald's bag.
But it's that much less.

I see my grandchildren's faces
And I worry about what world they are growing up in,
But I do see some things
That make me know
It could get better.

I see a new generation
Of kids who are offended by the word "Faggot"
As I was by the word "Nigger".

I see efforts being made
To repeal DOMA and DADT.
I see states rising for non-discrimination laws
Only a few, so far, but there are that few.

And once again, I remember.
I remember "NO Irish need apply"
I remember "Whites only"
I remember a shooting of 2 little girls in their church
And a march on Washington.
I remember friends killed in 'Nam
And friends running to Canada.

I remember Abraham, Martin and John,
Not to mention Bobby.
His funeral wreaths were in my first wedding picture--
Omens, much...?

And I remember
That "my country"
Has always been this way,
A mix of dreadful and wonderful,
Some things to kiss the ground about,
And others to kick the politicians and warmongers about.

And so--
What can I do?
Nothing except
What I am doing.
Be myself,
Speak my truth,
Act where I can,
Try,
Think,
Write,
Speak,
Pray--
And most of all,
Be real.

And give thanks
For those things
I do see happening,
And refuse to despair
Over those which haven't happened
Yet.
Because,
As I can testify
From 63 years of living,
They will.

No hatemonger or doomsayer
Or negative journalist
Is going to form my thoughts
No one is going to make me cease to believe.

This is still America,
It is still my country.
It is still America the Beautiful
And if I do not give up
It can still
Get better.

I Can't Stand It!   *(form: Dramatic Monologue)*

Oh, fuck off, you thrice-imbecilic moron!
Not a word of what you're saying will I hear...
"La, la, la, la"...I'm paying no attention,
At any time you get your daily bore on.
See! Look! I have a finger in each ear.
No ear-room will I give you! Not to mention

That I will use the newspaper in which
You rant your addled, boring propaganda
To line my bird cage. Wait, I have no bird.
So maybe it's the catbox where I'll ditch
Your noxious taradiddle. If you wondah
Why I do this, then perhaps you haven't heard--

Your game is out of fashion. You're a bore.
You're slinging anti-immigration hate
As well as homophobic rhetoric,
And I don't want to hear it any more.
How long will normal people have to wait
Before you realize, you make us sick?

I'll hear you no more. Now, I take a stand!
No more Faux News, no hate sites, no more signs
Or rallies by Fred Phelps and all his kind.
Here, asshole, let me take you by the hand,
And shove you out the door. I'm drawing lines
To keep you out, of my sight, life, and mind.

It Gets Better (form: The Bop)

They're yelling at him again, down the hall.
I can hear it from my classroom where I sit
Correcting papers, trying not to hear.
Once more the yelling. This time with the sound
Of someone crashing into someone's locker.
"Faggot!" "Pansy!" "Girlfriend, you're so GAY!"

I wish I dared to tell him...it gets better.

At last, it's quiet down there. Just the sound
Of footsteps running swift the other way.
I guess the janitor has just come in
The door from the back yard. And so they ran,
As cowards always run. Their battered prey
Whose name I do not know, is left behind
And I can hear him now, a quiet sound
Of sniffling, as he walks the other way...

I wish I dared to tell him, "It gets better".

He'll come right past my door. He won't come in.
No one can see him, not until he can
Become a man again. And I? I know
If I 'come out' to him, or anyone,
I'll lose this job. No question. So, I can't.
I hope someday he'll have a life, a mate.

I wish I dared to tell him...it gets better.

I am a lesbian. But no one knows.
I've taught here seven years. And when I leave
I go home to my house, my wife, my cats,
My comfortable life. I am much loved.
I still can't be myself here at the school
But everywhere else, I am truly ME.

I wish I dared to tell him. It. Gets. Better.

I Cry Out To The Rock....

Oh, strong, stalwart stone,
O thou upon whom was built
The foundation of history,
The church of Jesus,
The bones of civilization,
Hear now my complaint of thee....

Thou has become a bulwark,
A symbol of fortitude,
An icon of stability,
The metaphor for firmness,
Unchangeability,
Those things which must BE.

I say unto thee now,
It is time to change that.
It is the time for you
To crumble, to become sand,
To give in to the vicissitudes
Of time, and wear, and growth.

Let a tree's roots crack you.
Let thunder shake you in your bed.
Let a bolt of lightning
Split you asunder.
Let yourself be Moved,
Changed, Dissolved, Remade.

Become the Living Stone,
The avatar of existence
From which all things were made.
Become again sentient,
Let yourself be a live thing,
A life form, one which grows.

Too long have we poor humans
Used you as a symbol
To excuse our own failures,
Our own mental laziness,
Our own stubborn wrong-headedness,
Our failures to Become.

So, O Rock, show us now
That you are bone of bone,
And bone must grow, or die.
Illustrate for us
The power of transformation,
The reality of malleability.

Make us aware
That it is not the Rock
Upon which we build
But the vitality of the structure
That will sustain us,
That will make us Beings.

O rock, I know you hear me.
Rise up now, in power.
Become an earthquake.
Open a chasm
Prove to us that you can change.
And then, we can, too.

Looking For Integrity *(form: Villanelle)*

It doesn't seem integrity has worth.
No more the "public servant" touts our needs;
More valued is the bloated purse's girth.

Dark comedy reflects their bitter mirth,
Bleak politics gives reason for their greeds;
It doesn't seem integrity has worth.

Not only has dishonour given birth
To soiled campaigns, but no one votes on 'deeds';
More valued is the bloated purse's girth.

Now corporations speak as persons. Dearth
Of values, meaning, substance, haunts their screeds.
It doesn't seem integrity has worth.

We watch as government spreads o'er the earth.
No wholesome food this grazing monster feeds;
More valued is the bloated purse's girth.

And those who hunger, given a wide berth
As famine to our land's destruction speeds.
It doesn't seem integrity has worth.
More valued is the bloated purse's girth.

Making It Up...

Sometimes I don't trust my own instincts
Sometimes I think I'm full of crap.
Sometimes I get so overloaded
Sometimes there's too much in my lap--

Sometimes I despair when I look at
The things I have promised to do.
Sometimes I am certain I'll never
Have the energy to see it through.

Sometimes I outsmart myself. Often
I can't find the next step to take.
Sometimes I am certain that next time
I pick up the load it will break.

And then I remember the magic
I learned when I danced as a girl.
If you step wrong, you're losing your balance,
You'll stay right-side-up if you twirl.

If you're there on the stage and can't think of
The next step to take, well, just take it.
If you float gracefully through an error
No one will notice you make it.

So when I am too overloaded,
When there's far too much wine in my cup,
When I'm stuck on the stage with no options,
I have one. I just make it up

Promise

Windowless faces, bleak with suffering,
Reflecting no light from eyes gray with poverty
Gaze sullenly at my smile,
With a kind of hunger no boon can assuage.

The repetitive torture of one more queue,
One more open admission that one is inadequate,
Contributes to the autism of homelessness,
World where there is nothing to say, no one to talk to.

All the human indignity of a lifetime of hunger
Swept into a pile too small to pick up,
Crumpled detritus of what used to be persons,
Resolving invisibly into meaningless lists of numbers.

We must remember
Their health is our health too.
If we cannot bring light back to those eyes,
We are blinder than they.

No More Listening...

33

Once I believed

In the infallibility

Of shining adult figures

Against the sometimes-brilliant sun.

Whenever such a one would speak

I thought the dictum applicable

To whatever bit of forgotten wisdom

My child-self had forgotten to live by.

"Eat your vegetables""Don't tease your sister"

"Go to church""Obey your auntie"--

Matronly posturing beneath feathered hats,

Face-powder caked in benevolent chins,

They spoke, always, as from heaven

And I listened. And I believed.

Now, I notice only the absence

Of the papers of authority

Whenever such a bloated figure opines.

Never do they speak the only truth I wish to hear;

"Don't listen to me.""Think for yourself"

Where We At?

No one really wants to be here,
In this morass of negativity and finger-pointing.
(and the word "morass" is just perfect,
incorporating, as it does, 'more' and 'ass'
which is what the people feel like, here).

So...where is this awful place?
I dunno...I was just looking at the map
And it doesn't seem to be listed anywhere.
Seems as if it's somewhere else,
And you can't get there from here.

So how on earth did we end up here?
I think we took a wrong turn back up the road,
Somewhere between "patriotism" and "civility",
And now we find ourselves lost in this swamp
Out here in the middle of absolutely nowhere.

How do we get ourselves out of here?
I am not sure that we can. It would require
Actually working together, listening to each other.
Maybe a venture into the byways of civility.
Looks like we're going to stay out here, lost.

Where we at, anyway?
No one knows.
But I want to go home.

Songs of My Heart

About The Harp

It breathes.
I feel it, nestled against me,
breathing my breath
before I strike a note.

Living it sings
With a voice
Larger than my hands,
Deeper than my heart,
Higher than my dreams.

Seeing it stand there
Is sheathed potential.
Arrow-strings taut, tensed at any sky,
It is a Now,
A Doing,
Unlike any other place or being.

I stretch
to reach all the strings
And feel life beneath my fingers
Unexpected
because I have not made it,
Engendered it.
It is its own,
Not mine.

It breathes there
It lives in the soul of former musics
Calling, crooning

Sleepsong
Griefsong
Laughtersong

And that other song
Self song
the one I play when no one is listening.

It is a place,
A time,
A history,
A Universe

How can people say
"the harp is so relaxing"
When within its voice
Are children and battles,
Wars and kingdoms
Births and alliances...

And yet it cradles me
like a lover
And sings songs
I never knew until it spoke.

Harp
Is a verb.

Cobalt

They are everywhere.
Shelves, bookcases, windowsills.
Inescapable.

They are scintillant,
Deep, lustrous,a quiet flame
Yet not obtrusive.

They call to the eye,
Silent, patient, insistent,
Not to be ignored.

They will pull you in,
Memories, reflections, gifts,
Places I have been.

They are my symbols
Of blue shimmering silence
At the heart of life.

Dark As Lightning

It shatters,
Enveloping the darkness
In momentary light.

The bolt brilliant,
Electric

Across the swathe of sky
Far darker than the land below
It stutters, hesitates,

Then rips a wall
Of electric astonishment
From horizon to horizon
Across the sea.

The camera lens,
Poor, paltry thing,
Too slow, too late,
Too feeble.

Nowhere near enough juice
To record the impetuous exclamation
Of the mother of all juice...

I find myself wondering
How often
Light, thrown in suddenness
Over the bleeding darkness
Of long-entrenched ideas

May serve only
To leave its dazzled spectators

More in the dark than before.

Curse or Blessing

Craggy-faced as the rocks,
He stood, rooted firm on the shore,
His back to the waters.

It was not his Land,
He, a Frenchman, no son of Eirinn,
But, he did not care.

In a whisper, he muttered,
While waving his hands in the air,
Maledictions, in French.

'Twas the Auld Ones he cursed,
The draiocht, the fili, the Land,
In the Name of his God.

Waves lapped at his heels.
He noticed, but calmly ignored;
His work was important.

His words fell to silence.
He spun, with a flip of his robes,
And re-entered the boat.

As the oarsmen took oars,
He turned for a pitying look
At the shores he had damned.

No more would the Snakes
Of draiocht and evil designing
Soil Eriu's fair face.

Twixt water and sand,
A ribbon of wrack in the waves
Formed a Guardian rune.

His shadow grew short
As the boat crested waves in the dusk,
Crossed the horizon.

Behind him, the Land
And the Folk, and the Druids he'd cursed
Watched as he left.

And yet, he returns,
Every year, cause for drinking, for dance,
An icon of Ireland.

It's an irony, this.
When you think how the things that he cursed
Now flourish, reborn.

The Druids still live,
All the Gods celebrated by Pagans,
Immrama still dreamt.

And Lá Fhéile Pádraig,
A holiday marking his coming
But not about God.

So, raise him a glass,
This man, who in bringing a curse
Brought "Erin go bragh!"

A chance to be proud
Of our Land, of our kith, of ourselves.
Just hear the Snakes laugh.

Double Meaning

I remember her kindness
In my moment of deepest sorrow...
She did not know how her words,
Casually passed over the counter
With a double latte
Made me feel as if it were possible
To once again feel joy.
Her ignorance was unintended,
However--far from "bliss"...
"Lost some weight around the waist, eh?"
She smiled and took my money,
And I turned and left.
Sometimes the memory slips back into my mind.
An intended compliment on my slimming,
Unknowing of the reason,
A babe, now gone forever.

Dumb Supper

I remember, on Samhain,
His laugh. Her smile. Their love.
The threshold gleams,
The fire is alive with eyes.
Souls join us at the table,
Once again we share words.
Midnight beckons, the blood sings.
Where I am, you once were.
Where you are, I shall be.
A murder of crows
In the moon-black night
Takes our offering.
The gates are open.
Death waits.
We will meet again.

Dust In The Word

Poets are the custodians
Of the Dustmites of the Universe.

There is no remedy for our condition.

We may be placed in verbal restraints
Such as L33tspeak, character limits, and illiterate texting--

Nevertheless, the infection has no difficulty
Permeating our appropriate body parts
And ruining our friendships
With anyone who does not think in iambs
And knows not that most slogans are pentameter.

Forgetfulness is the idiom of the non-poet,
But we are cursed with never-forgetfulness.

We notice everything. Dustmites. Crumbs. Inconsistency.
And once noticed, it becomes poem-fodder.

That way, no one else will ever forget it, either.

Hoodie Crow

She is screeching down the hollow echoes of your shattered mind,
She is clawing with her talons at the wraith you cannot find
For her power has destroyed it, and it 'ere no more can be
And you bleed, and coil, and crumble, as her power sets it free.

You are powerless to stop her, she is clawing at your eyes
And her own are black obsidian, immune to your disguise,
For despite your craven cringing as you run and try to hide
The crow has marked your path and will destroy you from inside.

Never seek to try evading, never dare to lift your hand
In retaliation, for her strength you never will withstand,
As she swoops in screaming majesty to tear your tattered face
And her wings are swirling whirlwinds to erase you from this place.

You are gone, destroyed, defeated, and the shrieking of her glee
Is the last humiliation of your pride, and sets her free,
Both herself and one she cares for, her beloved, wife, and pet,
And for all your naked suffering, you always will regret

Having meddled in the business of the Witch who lays this curse,
And despite the dread you now must feel, it only will get worse.
For her power is supreme and in its working she's the queen...
And there's nought for you to do but bow, and, broken, flee the scene..

In The Belly

She quivers behind my lips all winter,
Never speaking, but filling my mind
With words unuttered,
Thoughts of poesy in silence,
Postponed for warmer days.

She dances in my old limbs,
Never moving, but filling my veins
With warm blood,
Making me wish for days long gone
When I was the night-dancer.

She lives inside my thoughts,
Never acting, but filling my head
With bard's fire,
Sparks of imbas, stored up,
To burst forth in springtime.

She flows in my stilled hands,
Never crafting, but filling my fingers
With stored skill,
Plans for drawing, painting, writing
All for later execution.

And then it comes...
La Fheile Brid, filling my Being
With Herself, Her Inspiration,
Her Creative Spark,
Her Healing Waters,
Her Ringing Song...

Brighid is coming!
Brighid is coming!
Brighid is here!
And I am no longer
In the belly....

Welcome Brighid....
All this you have given me,
All this which comes forth,
All this is Yours...
As am I.

Into The Mist

The trees are sinister
Ragged edges of fog
Like tattered cobweb-fingers
Beckoning eerily

Between the hummocks,
Tiny rivulets
Of unnamed water
Not flowing...perhaps waiting.

The air is alive.
Dank, resonant,
Hollowly echoing
Cries stilled before forming.

I stand at forest's edge
Not able to move
Nor to stand still.
Pulled in, scarcely knowing...

Where will it lead me?
The mist is leering,
A dank scent like tired hollows
Filled with nameless, moving things...

I must not enter.
I cannot stay here.
I cannot continue down this path.
I cannot prevent my going...

Is this how it feels?
Is the end of all simply this grey nothing?
Am I simply going to be absorbed here?
Is there nothing but this mist?

No one answers
No sound.
My hands are disappearing.
My eyes are dimming.
Where am I?

Moon Mother

We stood last night, a circle of kindred, and watched Her
Coming out from behind the crag of Mt. Olympus

Not shy, this globe of glowing silver light,
But plangent, full and bursting, assertive, a Presence.

She was THERE....and we....?

We stood, cups in hand, watching the unveiling
Sight seen so often, never taken for granted,
Her bounteous presence once again with us,
And yet new, unexpected, ever vivid and compelling
like the air you breathe every morning,
essential and appreciated,
though often unremarked.

But we had to mark Her, this night, this appearance...
It was like the processional of an ancient Queen,
Panoplied in splendor, golden, coruscating, glinting with awareness...
She would not be unregarded.

And we raised our cups, and honored Her, and bowed....
None of us, we urban-dwelling Pagans,
even for a moment thinking of Science or Technology,
But all of us awed once again, as our race has been from time immemorial,
By the living presence of the Lady,
The Mother of Lights,
In Her silvered radiance.

She is a Mystery, and we watch in awe,
As her face reveals itself to us again and again,
Always for the first time.

We drank deep, mead we had made together, and savored the moment...
Ancient wine, ancient Lady, ancient mystery of craft and kith,
Loving our Presence here in timelessness
within the globe of silver light,
And still so essentially present in our own world,
The hiss of cars on the motorway resonating with the pulse of crashing surf,
Recalled in genetic memory, though never experienced.

And at that moment, we recalled
Or thought for the first time,
Of all the Hidden Children,
over our land and other lands

All of them watching
Seeing Her in radiance,
The same glowing silver face
The same breathless awakening,
The same Awe,

Time and place compelling different circumstances
But all kindred, honoring the Mother of All.

We lifted our glasses again,
Gazing ever upward,
And felt our connection
To those unknown faces,
Perhaps also raising glasses in tribute.

We drank to them
A toast to "the Others"
Her other children,
Those we will never see,
But whom we Know,
More intimately, perhaps, than those
with whom we brush careless shoulders
In offices and stores
Where her face does not shine.

We connected
In moonlight
to all those we may never see,
But whose hearts and minds are kin to us
because of Her shining silver radiance,

And She smiled.

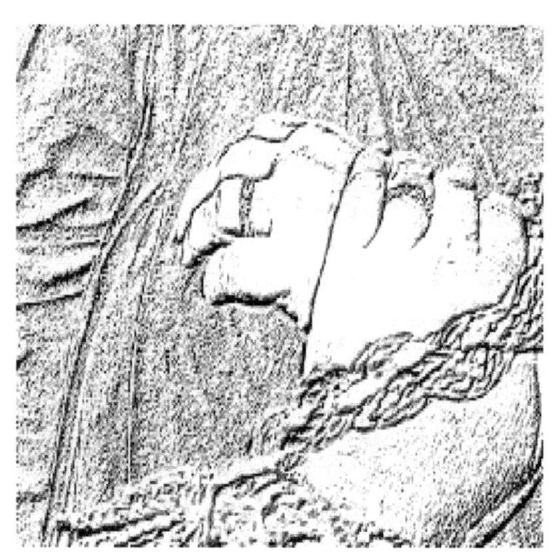

Not Dancing At Lughnassadh

I used to dig camping.
Now--I have issues.

Can't sleep on the ground--
Where's there a tent with a recliner in it?

Love the outdoors
But allergic to bugs.
That gorgeous dragonfly might be one exception.

I am obsessed with the raven,
Squawking his joy at his recent wedding
In the tree overhead--
But he's keeping me awake.

That last log you put on the fire
Ate my last marshmallow--but that's ok.
Now I can't eat sweets any more, anyway.

I'm so glad there's a campout by the lake--
But I'm not going.

I'll just sit here in comfort
In Mah Chayuh
In front of the swamp cooler
And look at the pictures.

Once More, With Feeling

Brighid, again....
Once more, with feeling,
Once more, Her festival.
Once more.

Brighid Duffy of Kildare,
My long-beloved ancestress,
Daughter of Duffy,
As am I.

An unique woman,
Unlike any other of her time.
"Not like other young things"
Said the poem.

She wanted to marry God.
She thought she was special,
She thought she had something to offer
And she did.

Look at this world,
Thousands of years later.
Everywhere, all over the globe
We know her name.

She is Springtime.
She is snowdrops
Blooming in the snow.
She is Hope.

She is Barding,
She is creating something
Where nothing was before.
She is Song.

She is Making,
She is using hands and heart
To make the world better.
She is Craft.

She is Healing.
She is waters of comfort
Flowing over bruised flesh.
She is Love.

On this day
The sun shines brightly
Onto melting snow.
It is Her day.

And she gifts us
With the sound of water
Snow melting, rain falling,
Life returning.

I will sing today.
I will do something loving.
I will make something new.
I will praise Her.
I have written
This poem, in the morning
On Her day
And for Her.

Brigid, my Mother,
My Ancestress, My Goddess
My inner Fire,
My Harpsong...

Burn bright.
Dance today, old limbs joyful
Sing with me
Voice rich and full.

Create with me,
Something new and lovely,
Making beauty
Where was none

It is Your Day.
I praise You
Once more,
With feeling.

Peace is within you.

It is not a gift that can be given by another person,
or a place, or a set of circumstances.
It is your birthright. It is your natural state of being.
It is your inalienable natural right to harmony
as you take your organic place in the world.

Peace is within you.

It can never be reft from you by circumstances.
It cannot be destroyed by war, or quarrelling,
or any disharmony that is sourced outside the Self.
It is the place Within where the Self finds refuge,
and that Place is unreachable by outside circumstances.

Peace is within you.

It is a deliberate, intentional choice of serenity
amidst a sea of chaos.
It is a conscious decision
to remain whole in the face of disintegration.
It is an affirmation of the Rightness of your Being.
It is the state at which your being finds equilibrium.
It is your Center.

Peace is within you.

It is not subject to the vicissitudes of living.
It cannot be broken, nor stolen,
nor in any way can that jewel of quietude
be removed from the inner core of your Self.

Peace is within you.

Even if you choose to ignore it,
it waits there at your Center,
peace essential, awaiting your rediscovery
of this undeniable Truth of human existence.

Peace is within you.

You are made of Beauty.
Your inheritance is Harmony.
You are a Gift of Life to the Universe.
You are essential to existence.
You cannot be beaten or bent or broken
by anything outside yourself.

Peace is within you.

There is a reason we use the term "Be AT Peace."
It is a place. It is a destination.
It is immediately, immanently, numinously,
within your reach. Right here. Right now.

Peace is within you.

Be....AT....Peace

Ritual

She always lights the candles first.
She always thinks of them as guardians,
She always picks the colors carefully.
She always remembers to smudge the altar.
She always uses a clean altar cloth,
She always meditates first.
She always invokes the goddess, and then the god.
She always does it on Monday nights,
She always remembers to turn off the phone.
She always has milk and cookies afterwards,
She always steps on the cat when she stands up.
She always writes down the date and time and intent in her BOS.
She always puts it on her calendar in her iPod.
She always knows where the Moon is.

She always tells herself it will be different this time.

She always wonders why nothing ever happens.

Samhain Fire

We stand around the circle,
the warmth penetrating.

The chill at centre is never fully thawed.

Our fingers are growing warmer.
Our hearts are shivering.

We are clinging to one another,
even if not actually touching.

We are lost in our own space,
each of us 'other' here,
no one connected,
floating between the worlds,
waiting for the dead.

The fire is alive now,
as the ancient folk saw it.

It is full of eyes,
watching, blinking,
Staring back boldly,
or evading our own eyes....

A Being, not a thing.
Sentient, watchful, omnivorous.
For some grinning, for others glaring.

No one is indifferent.

There is no such thing as 'not believing,'
Not for us,
Witches who wait, knowing,

Not here
on the threshold of darkness.

The World falls away
into infinite nothingness,
and we reach, just a little,
hoping through the flames
to grasp a spectral hand
or perhaps catch a fleeting glimpse
of features once beloved,
now turning away in silence.

We are not daunted
by the crackling of flames
echoing in infinite space.

Within each of us is a spark
connected to that fire...

The road through the flames beckons,
seductive, yet harrowing,
luring with molten glow
those of us, waiting and watchful,

Each wondering at deepest core,
who will next walk through those flames,
who might, by this time next year,
be on the other side of that glowing horizon,
looking back.

Not young, we.
Not foolish.
Aware of all the risks of living,

Embracing them, gladly,
for the knowledge
of life and love
that comes with breath.

and yet, at Samhain,
we fear,
and tremble,
knowing that whatever awaits us
beyond the flames,
it is a Mystery.

No one,
for all our ken and cunning,
has been past this threshold.

We wait, wary,
shivering within ourselves,
alone, albeit together,
conscious of one another's shoulders,
but not of one another's souls.

The Fire glows on,
Unstinting, full and flowering,
A gateway and a barrier,

Threshold of soul's rest
for all who may pass,
straitly forbidding the living,
even on this night of access.

We may stand here
until we root to the ground.

Or we may turn
on trembling legs
and seek comfort and shelter
and the warm food of life.

Fire remains.

Glowing indifferently,
living on the air we breathe,
feeding on the silent night.

It will wait us out.

SILENCE...

66

...so different from "quiet"...
      there is texture in silence,
  and movement,
     and feeling...
there is tension and release
the inside
 of a large, cool sphere,
   green water,
     blue rain,
      gold light...
the whirr of business...
  busy.....ness....

all the movement echoes....
  all the strings are muted.....

"hush"is such a pretty word,
    a crystal word...
you can pour light out of your hands
     like water...

...you touch air...
    ..you breathe life....
     the sun shines through your hand,
      and the bones slide
       and the blood dances....

...conscious of me--- i --- small letter....
    a separate creation--
     a part of Creation...
all moving and real and Alive...
    and all that is...
     ....Is....

unafraid of the wasps,
        as neither of us intrudes....
they breathe their universe,
        i mine...
we share life...
        we notice, but do not mark,
            one another....

...the mechanical world...
        not intrusion,
                completion....
an airplane right as a birdsong
        in time, space,
silence to hear them both....

...one speaks to the world
        in silence only...
words retard communication....
        the stillness shimmers,
strings of silk...

the sound of one heart beating
        is the pulse
            of the world.....

Snowfall on My Garden--A Meditation

Beneath a blanket

Of crystallized memory

They sleep in ignorance,

Scarcely remembering

The barren dreamlessness

Of this long night of waiting--

I draw from this

My own conclusions

As my mind branches forth

To newer, fresher ideas

Not crystalline, not frozen

But fresh and green--

There is a difference between

Waiting to die

And living.

Age does not need to mean oblivion.

Conundrum

I will never understand
The primeval urge
To gaze so far beyond
The current circumstance
That the fulfillment
Of this very waking moment
In all its untrammeled glory
Never comes to fruition.

We are enabled
By a magical gift
To reap the essence
Of each moment of living.
Why are we so hungry
For empty reassurance
About what is to follow?
Why can't we just live--NOW?

Imagine

Imagine a man who knows that the God lives within him and takes joy in that,
A man who has spent his entire life becoming who he Is,
One who knows the truest test of manhood is the ability to evolve.

Imagine a man who is truly made in the image and likeness of the God.
A man who knows the difference between strength and bullying--
One who knows that big boys do, too, cry...

Imagine a man who listens as much to others as he does to himself,
A man who truly listens to himself--his High Self--
One who knows that sometimes the best thing to say is the gift of silence.

Imagine a man who is not afraid to be gentle.
A man who knows that men, too, deserve the full realm of emotion.
One who laughs and thinks, and isn't always a "tough guy."

Imagine a man who remembers the lessons of his youth,
A man who recalls what it was like to be the smallest, the youngest--
One who gifts the young men in his life with what he wishes he had received.

Imagine a man who does not define himself by his job,
A man who knows "what do you do" is less a question than "what do you believe",
One who has made a career out of loving him Self.

Imagine a man who honours the Spirit of the Goddess
A man who does not think of men and women as the first and second sex--
One who reveres the influence of mother, sister, wife and friend.

Imagine a man who chooses his friends as more than "drinking buddies",
A man who learns from fathers, brothers, husbands, to become more, better--
One who strives to make the world a better place for all men.

Imagine yourself as this man.

Crystal Dreaming

Welcome to the Miracle--

As you enter the door,

You grow thoughtful

At the perfect symmetry

Of the inside of the ruby crystal.

A touch as soft

As the kiss of a baby

Brushes your lips.

You reach forward

Into crimson fire,

And gasp with amazement

As the heart of the crystal pulses.

In a split-second,

You annihilate

A billion fears.

You are filled with scarlet light.

You sleep.

Through the Looking-Glass

This endeavor could,
We feared,
Permanently disrupt
The timeline,
Creating profound unrest
In the fourth realm.

None of us knew,
As we gazed in the mirror,
How close to the edge
Our hesitant look
Into the future
Might move us.

From my chair,
I saw the darkness,
As the captain,
A man of petty quibbling
Said to us, "Look! Stop!
It's dangerous!"
    So I jumped.

Space Within Me *(form: Paradelle)*

Go within to find the sense of Self
Go within to find the sense of Self
Inner space holds secrets undefined--
Inner space holds secrets undefined.
Within, find of inner secrets to Self,
Undefined, the space holds sense. Go.

Sit in contemplation, mind at rest,
Sit in contemplation, mind at rest.
Open heart, the soul resides in silence,
Open heart, the soul resides in silence.
Rest in contemplation. At the soul,
Sit, Heart. Silence resides in open Mind.

Never close the gates that lead within.
Never close the gates that lead within,
For, beyond, the universe spreads wide.
For, beyond, the universe spreads wide.
For close beyond Never, within the gates
That lead wide, the Universe spreads...

Witches Pyramid

To know...that one was easiest...
To my peril, because I became arrogant...
And indeed, the pyramid collapsed
With the weight of my over-confidence.

So once again, I began to build.
To know.
Not to tell everyone everything.
Not to brag, or boast, or blather.
But to quietly, successfully,
Go about the Work,
And the final result
Would come in its time
Successfully
This I know.

And so, **to Will**
To do more than Want
But to intend, to focus,
Indeed, to Be the thing desired.
When did I finally realize
That Willing is not something you do,
And Willing is not something you want.
The True Will is Who You Are...
And I know this.
And I am this.

And so, **to Dare.**
Reaching beyond the Self
To encounter the Being of the Other,
Others, people, sisters, brothers, friends.
To Dare, to speak one's Truth
To Dare, to be in another's grief
To Dare, to change, to become, to be More
More than Self
More than Will
Daring, and Sharing
And becoming One.

And so, to the final rung
The final angle of the Pyramid.
Now I Am With...
Now there is We, not just I
Now I see, and I hear
In the hearts, in the pain
In the crisis and the struggle of the Other
I am there
I am Daring to Be
With the Other,
Joined,
Friend, Brother, Sister, Lover, Companion.

And so, we are One.
And so, I see through the eyes of others.
I see hatred,
I see dishonor,
I see injustice,
I see lies that hurt.

And so....here, now, on that fourth angle
One step from completing the Pyramid.
I halt.
I have to stop.
I cannot continue.

For here and now,
In the pain of the Other
Who is also mySelf,
In the grip of injustice,
How can I **Be Silent?**

www.ingramcontent.com/pod-product-compliance
Lightning Source LLC
Chambersburg PA
CBHW061035050726
47592CB00004B/1446